ULTIMATE X-MEN

THE TOMORROW PEOPLE

MARK MILLAR
Writer

ADAM KUBERT
Pencils

ART THIBERT, DANNY MIKI & JOE WEEMS
Inks

RICHARD ISANOVE
Colours

RS & COMICRAFT's WES ABBOTT
Letters

MARK POWERS
Editor

PETE FRANCO
Assistant Editor

JOE QUESADA
Editor in chief

ADAM KUBERT
Cover art

MARVEL GRAPHIC NOVEL presents ULTIMATE X-MEN: THE TOMORROW PEOPLE

Contains material originally published in magazine form as ULTIMATE X-MEN issues 1-6.
Published by Panini Publishing, a division of Panini UK Limited. Mike Riddell, Managing Director. Alan O'Keefe, Managing Editor. Mark Irvine, Production Manager. Marco M. Lupoi, Publishing Director, Europe. Marcello Riboni, Project Leader. Alessandra Gozzi, Pre-press manager. Roberto Rubbi, Design Manager. Office of Publication: Panini House, Coach & Horses Passage, The Pantiles, Tunbridge Wells, Kent, TN2 5UJ. Tel: 01892 500 100. Copyright: © 2001, 2003 by Marvel Characters, Inc. All rights reserved. No similarity between any of the names, characters, persons and/or institutions in this book with those of any living or dead person or institution is intended, and any such similarity which may exist is purely coincidental. This publication may not be sold except by authorized dealers and is sold subject to the conditions that it shall not be sold or distributed with any part of its cover or markings removed, nor in a mutilated condition. ULTIMATE X-MEN (including all prominent characters featured in this issue and the distinctive likenesses thereof) is a trademark of MARVEL CHARACTERS, INC. and this publication is under license from Marvel Characters, Inc. thru Panini S.p.A. Printed in Italy. ISBN 1-904159-13-3

The TOMORROW PEOPLE

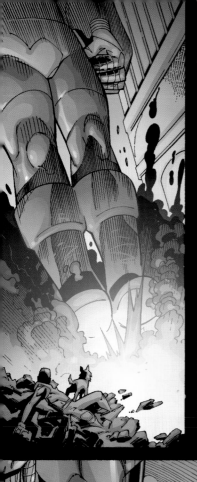

ΓΗΒΥ–7–8888–ΦΤΨ95
ΗΗΓΗΞΧΦΓΞΡ999–9875

Mutant Gene CONFIRMED
Proceed with TERMINATION

ΚΦΣ.Κ
Λ–/9΄/99~
0897Β–ΒΒΝε
ΙΟΟCΟΙΟΟΙΙΙΙΟΙΟΙΟΙΟΟΟΙΟΙ
Μ ΓΗΚΦΒ–98/Τ435

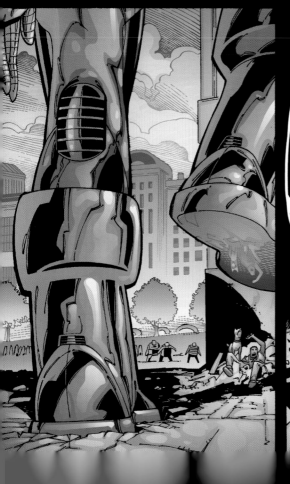

CRUNCH

MUTANT NEST IN L.A.

GOOD EVENING: I'M **BOAZ ESHELMEN** AND YOU'RE WATCHING THE CHANNEL NINE **NEWS UPDATE.**

TONIGHT'S TOP STORY: TRIAL RUN OF **THE SENTINELS** IS HAILED AS A TRIUMPHANT **SUCCESS** AS A MUTANT NEST IN LOS ANGELES IS UNCOVERED AND NEUTRALIZED WITH **NO** CIVILIAN CASUALTIES.

WERE THESE MUTANT TERRORISTS BEHIND THE RECENT ANTI-HUMAN BOMBINGS IN **NEW YORK** AND **WASHINGTON?** POLICE SAY THE EVIDENCE IS **UNDENIABLE** --

-- BUT HUMAN RIGHTS CAMPAIGNERS AMNESTY INTERNATIONAL HAVE CONDEMNED THE ACTION AS "**INHUMAN** AND **UNCONSTITUTIONAL,**" PROVOKING A STERN WHITE HOUSE RESPONSE --

HOW ANYONE CAN QUESTION THE SENTINEL INITIATIVE AFTER THE **WASHINGTON ANNIHILATION** IS ASTONISHING.

THE PRESIDENT WISHES TO REAFFIRM HIS SUPPORT FOR THIS PROJECT, AND OFFERS HIS MOST SINCERE **CONGRATULATIONS** TO THE FEDERAL EMPLOYEES BEHIND IT.

THE PRESIDENT'S PRESS SECRETARY WAS, OF COURSE, REFERRING TO THE **BROTHERHOOD OF MUTANTS'** DEVASTATING BOMB-BLAST ON CAPITOL HILL ONLY **SEVEN DAYS** AGO.

AND THE SUBSEQUENT BROADCAST FROM **MAGNETO,** MASTER OF **MAGNETISM** -- THE DEATH CULT'S SELF-APPOINTED **LEADER...**

MAN IS A PARASITE UPON MUTANT **RESOURCES**. HE EATS OUR **FOOD**, BREATHES OUR **AIR** AND OCCUPIES LAND WHICH EVOLUTION INTENDED **HOMO SUPERIOR** TO INHERIT.

NATURALLY, OUR ATTACKS UPON YOUR POWER BASES WILL CONTINUE UNTIL YOU DELIVER THIS WORLD TO ITS **RIGHTFUL** OWNERS.

BUT YOUR REPLACEMENTS GROW **IMPATIENT**.

FORMER **NASA** ENGINEER AND SENTINEL DESIGNER, PROFESSOR **BOLIVAR TRASK**, WAS PLEASED WITH THE PERFORMANCE OF HIS ANDROIDS, AND IS EXCITED ABOUT **FUTURE POTENTIAL** --

WE'VE LIVED IN FEAR OF THE **MUTANTS** FOR AS LONG AS I CAN REMEMBER, BUT TODAY GOES DOWN IN HISTORY AS THE TURNING POINT WHERE **ORDINARY PEOPLE** STARTED FIGHTING BACK.

LOS ANGELES WAS ONLY THE FIRST STEP: MY COLLEAGUES AND I ESTIMATE THAT EVERY MUTANT HIDING IN THE UNITED STATES WILL BE **DETAINED** WITHIN THE NEXT SIX TO EIGHT WEEKS.

A LITTLE BIRDY INFORMS ME THAT EVERY CENT YOU'RE PAID BY THE RUSSIAN MAFIA GETS WIRED BACK TO YOUR IMPOVERISHED FAMILY ON SIBERIA, MR. RASPUTIN.

I WONDER, ARE *ALL* SOVIET EXPATRIATES SUCH MOTHER'S BOYS, OR IS THIS BEHAVIOR EXCLUSIVE TO THE ARMS-DEALING COMMUNITY?

JUST SHUT UP AND CHECK THE MERCHANDISE BEFORE I KICK YOU IN THE NUTS SO HARD YOU'RE GULPING WITH *THREE* ADAM'S APPLES, AHMED.

YOUR KGB SUITCASE-NUKE LOOKS QUITE IN ORDER, YOUNG MAN.

I BELIEVE THE GENTLEMAN I REPRESENT WILL BE *MOST* SATISFIED.

MY THANKS FOR SUCH A SMOOTH TRANSACTION, AND I'M CERTAIN WE SHALL DO BUSINESS AGAIN IN THE VERY NEAR *FUTURE*.

FREEZE, YOU LITTLE SNAKE. ISN'T IT CUSTOMARY WHERE YOU COM FROM TO LET A BUSINESS ASSOCIATE ACTUALLY COUNT THE MILLION DOLLARS IN EVERY MILLION-DOLLAR DEAL?

I'M AFRAID THAT DEPENDS ENTIRELY ON WHETHER THEY'VE JUST BEEN HANDED A SUITCASE FULL OF *MONOPOLY MONEY*, MY DEAR, YOUNG FRIEND...

THERE'S NO DENYING YOU'VE GOT A BEAUTIFUL SCHOOL HERE, BUT WHAT KIND OF PRINCIPAL DESIGNS BLACK LATEX UNIFORMS FOR HIS IMPRESSIONABLE TEENAGE *STUDENTS*?

THE KIND WHO WANTS THE MUTANT GENE WE'RE ALL CARRYING AROUND TO REMAIN UNDETECTED BY THE SENTINELS, I'D IMAGINE.

THE UNIFORM IS A *CLOAKING DEVICE.* AS LONG AS YOU'RE WEARING ONE OF *THESE,* THE SENTINELS ARE FOOLED INTO THINKING YOUR BIO-SIGNATURE IS SAFELY IN THE *HUMAN* RANGE.

AREN'T YOU WORRIED THESE *PAINTERS* WILL TELL SOMEONE YOU'RE RUNNING A SAFEHOUSE FOR ILLEGAL MUTANTS?

YOU COULD FLY A *PLANE* DOWN THAT CORRIDOR AND THE POOR DEVILS WOULD BE CONVINCED THEY WERE LOOKING AT A *WASP.*

COME IN, MY FRIENDS. JOIN ME FOR A PERRIER IN THE LIBRARY.

UH, IS IT JUST *ME* OR IS THERE SOME CREEPY GUY TALKING DIRECTLY INTO OUR BRAINS ABOUT *WASPS?*

NOT IN THE *SLIGHTEST,* COLOSSUS. I PLACED THESE FINE GENTLEMEN IN A POST-HYPNOTIC TRANCE WHEN I HIRED THEM.

LADIES AND GENTLEMEN, A ROUND OF APPLAUSE FOR *THE ICEMAN*, PLEASE.

YOU JUST SPLIT HIS *HEAD* OPEN, YOU IDIOT!

GOOD! I HOPE HE'S *DEAD!* MAYBE THEN FREAKS LIKE *YOU* WILL FINALLY GET THE *MESSAGE!*

ARE YOU PEOPLE *INSANE?* THIS BOY JUST SAVED YOUR *LIVES!*

JEAN, LET IT GO. IT'S NOT WORTH IT.

JUST GET *OUT* OF HERE.

-- IT SEEMS OUR OLD FRIEND CHARLES XAVIER IS *ALIVE AND WELL,* GENTLEMEN.

AN ORGANIZED CELL OF OUTCASTS RISKING THEIR LIVES FOR A FEW GRINNING PRIMATES?

SERIOUSLY? I MEAN, I RECOGNIZED *JEAN GREY* AND A COUPLE OF THE *OTHERS* WE WERE AFTER, BUT I DIDN'T SEE *XAVIER* IN ANY OF THE NEWS FOOTAGE, MAGNETO.

CONTRARY TO WHAT WE MIGHT HAVE BELIEVED --

FWA

HE MIGHT AS WELL HAVE SIGNED THE BOTTOM OF THE SCREEN, *TOAD.*

THE ARMS DEALERS ARE WAITING UPSTAIRS, MAGNETO.

AH, THE FAT, LITTLE HOMO SAPIEN WHO MANAGED TO LOSE MY NUCLEAR WEAPON. TELL HIM TO WAIT IN THE MUSIC ROOM, QUICKSILVER.

I'M GOING TO WATCH THE VIDEOTAPE AGAIN.

WELL, I GUESS ANY DOUBTS WE HAD ABOUT THE AUTHENTICITY OF THAT TIP-OFF CAN BE DISMISSED, WOLVERINE.

THERE AIN'T MANY PEOPLE ON GOD'S GOOD EARTH WHO CAN TAKE A HUNDRED BULLETS IN THE RUMP AND WAKE UP WITH NOTHING WORSE THAN A *HANGOVER.*

WRAITH?

THAT'S RIGHT, SOLDIER.

WELCOME BACK TO *WEAPON X.*

TINK TINK TINK TI

WHOA. EASY, TIGER.

I'VE SEEN THOSE CLAWS TEAR THROUGH THE SIDE OF A TANK, BUT THAT CAGE IS MADE OF THE SAME SEMI-INDESTRUCTIBLE MATERIAL OUR DOCTORS LINED YOUR *BONES* WITH.

CUTTING LOOSE FROM THIS OUTFIT *ONCE* IS MORE THAN ANY MUTANT EVER MANAGED IN THE PAST, SON.

NOBODY GETS THAT LUCKY *TWICE* IN A LIFETIME.

KA-CHICT

POP!
POP!
POP!
POP!

POP

POP

SIR, WHAT ARE YOU *DOING*?

THE SAME THING WE USED TO DO EVERY NIGHT WHEN THERE WAS NOTHING GOOD ON T.V.

REMEMBER THE LAUGHS WE USED TO HAVE WITH THAT *HEALING FACTOR* OF YOURS, WOLVERINE?

YOU COULD SHOOT HIM, STAB HIM, CRACK HIS HEAD OPEN WITH AN IRON BAR -- HIS MUTANT HEALING ABILITY MEANT THAT HE COULD ALWAYS JUST PIECE HIMSELF BACK *TOGETHER* AGAIN.

HELL, BIG JIM GRANT EVEN DOUSED HIM IN GASOLINE AND SET HIM ALIGHT ONE TIME, AND HE WAS *STILL* UP FOR WEAPON X'S NICARAGUA OPERATION TWO DAYS LATER.

SHAME THE SAME COULDN'T BE SAID FOR THAT LITTLE SNOT WE HAD TO SCOOP UP IN THOSE PLASTIC BAGS AT THE AIRPORT.

YOU DIRTY SON OF A--

WATCH YOUR MOUTH, *MUTIE*.

POP!

WOW. NICE BIKE.

DON'T JUST STAND THERE CATCHING *FLIES* IN YOUR MOUTHS!

GET *AFTER* HIM!

C'MON, LIEBOWITZ! DOESN'T THIS THING GO ANY *FASTER*?!

COLONEL, I GO ANY *FASTER* AND I'LL PUT THE *GAS PEDAL* THROUGH THE *FLOOR.*

ALL I ASK IS THAT EXTRA TEN PERCENT, SOLDIER.

WAIT -- THERE'S SOMETHING UP AHEAD ON THE ROAD!

BOO.

HOLY S--

LIEBOWITZ?!
HOLY MOTHER OF GOD --! YOU JUST BROKE HIS FREAKIN' NECK!

LUCKY LIEBOWITZ.

WOLVERINE --
NO!
DON'T KILL HIM!

I CAN'T IMAGINE WHAT THAT ANIMAL PUT YOU THROUGH OVER THE YEARS, BUT MURDER HIM OUT HERE LIKE THIS AND ALL YOU'RE GOING TO DO IS PROVE THAT THE PAPERS ARE *RIGHT* ABOUT US.

BABE, DO I LOOK LIKE THE KIND OF GUY WHO LIES AWAKE AT NIGHT WORRYING ABOUT THE PUBLIC'S PERCEPTION OF MUTANTS?

YOU'VE HAD A *HARD ENOUGH* DAY, BIG MAN.

DON'T MAKE ME *HURT* YOU.

AND HOW DO YOU PROPOSE TO DO *THAT*, GORGEOUS?

HIT ME WITH A *HIGH-HEEL*? SMACK ME IN THE FACE WITH YOUR *BARBIE* PURSE?

THE TOMORROW PEOPLE

PART 3 OF 6

PROFESSOR X DOESN'T STRIKE ME AS THE KIND OF GUY WHO'D MAKE SOMETHING LIKE THAT UP FOR A LAUGH, ICEMAN.

WOW.

I THINK THAT DR. PEPPER I JUST HAD IS TRICKLING DOWN MY LEG.

THIS IS INSANE. WE SHOULDN'T HAVE TO LIVE LIKE THIS.

A COUPLE OF MONTHS AGO, I COULDN'T SLEEP BECAUSE I WAS WORRIED MY DAD WOULD FIND OUT I STOLE TWENTY BUCKS FROM HIS JACKET.

NOW I'M A SUSPECTED TERRORIST BECAUSE I'M CARRYING UNFASHIONABLE DNA.

THAT'S PROBABLY JUST HIS BLACK OPS TRAINING, STORM.

IF THERE WAS ANYTHING GENUINELY SINISTER GOING ON IN HIS HEAD, THE PROFESSOR WOULD BE THE FIRST TO KNOW ABOUT IT.

SUBWAY

THE ONLY GOOD MUTANT IS A DEAD MUTA

Mutie equals daddie

U SAID IT!

ARE YOU A HUNDRED PERCENT SURE THESE CLOTHES HIDE OUR MUTANT BIO-SIGNATURES FROM THE SENTINELS, *STORM?*

COLOSSUS AND I DON'T LIKE BEING HOLED UP IN XAVIER'S OLD SCHOOL EITHER, ICEMAN, BUT GOING SOLO JUST MEANS YOU END UP AS DEAD AS THE MUTANTS YOU SEE ON THE NEWS.

ACTUALLY, I'M STARTING TO *LIKE* THE SCHOOL.

IT'S FUN BEING AROUND PEOPLE WHERE I DON'T HAVE TO KEEP UP THAT LAME, HOMO SAPIEN PRETENSE.

OF COURSE, CYCLOPS CAN BE A LITTLE *INTENSE* SOMETIMES, BUT HE'S SURPRISINGLY FUNNY ONCE HE DROPS ALL THE BARRIERS.

SAME GOES FOR *BEAST* AND *MARVEL GIRL:* WHO *COULDN'T* LIKE A TELEPATH WHO FIRES DIRTY JOKES INTO YOUR HEAD WHEN PROFESSOR X IS BEING *SERIOUS?*

THE ONLY ONE I HAVEN'T REALLY WARMED UP TO YET IS *WOLVERINE.*

GOD, I *LOATHE* WOLVERINE. HAVE YOU SEEN THE WAY HE CHECKS EVERYONE OUT WITH THOSE MEAN, LITTLE EYES? IT'S LIKE HE'S SIZING US ALL UP FOR *COFFINS.*

I FEEL LIKE I'M CRACKING HEADS IN THE *SPINA BIFIDA* WARD HERE.

YOU BADLY-TRAINED *MORONS* WERE DEAD THE MINUTE YOU LOOKED ME IN THE EYE.

THE ONLY REAL QUESTION I HAD WAS WHETHER MY *ADAMANTIUM CLAWS* WERE TOUGHER THAN THIS RUSSIAN CLOWN'S *ORGANIC METAL SHELL*.

BUT I GUESS THE EIGHT PINTS OF *RHESUS NEGATIVE* SEEPING OUT ONTO THE GRASS ANSWERS THAT. RIGHT, PROFESSOR?

I'D BE LYING IF I SAID I WASN'T IMPRESSED ON SOME PRIMITIVE LEVEL, WOLVERINE --

-- BUT YOU'RE ONLY SUPPOSED TO **WRESTLE** YOUR FELLOW X-MEN IN THESE **DANGER ROOM** EXERCISES, NOT HACK THEM TO PIECES.

SORRY, BUB. FORCE OF HABIT.

THESE **VIRTUAL SIMULATIONS** YOU PUT TOGETHER ARE PRETTY **CONVINCING**, BEAST. YOU GOT ANY **OVER-18** VERSIONS?

CONSIDER YOURSELF AT THE TOP OF THE LIST FOR THE **BRITNEY AND CHRISTINA** PROGRAM I'VE BEEN WORKING ON UPSTAIRS.

I'M GLAD YOU'RE SETTLING IN, WOLVERINE, BUT I MUST ADMIT I'M A LITTLE SURPRISED YOU'VE **REMAINED** WITH US THIS LONG.

YEAH, WHAT ATTRACTS A MAVERICK WITH A REP LIKE YOURS TO OUR QUIET, LITTLE UPSTATE **SAFE HOUSE?**

CHARLES XAVIER IS OUR SINGLE **OBSTACLE**, WOLVERINE. I WANT YOU TO INFILTRATE HIS CIRCLE AND **ELIMINATE** HIM.

YOU'RE THE ONLY ONE AMONG US WHO CAN SHIELD HIS **THOUGHTS** AND THE ONE MAN ALIVE I CAN **TRUST** THIS MISSION TO.

THE SCENERY, BUB. THE SCENERY.

BUT RESCUING THE *FIRST DAUGHTER* OR WHATEVER THEY *CALL* HER, MEANS THE SENTINELS ARE GOING TO BE OUT THERE *FOREVER,* PROFESSOR.

I DON'T LIKE MAGNETO ANY MORE THAN *YOU* DO, BUT AT LEAST HE'S STOPPED THE GOVERNMENT FROM KILLING *MUTANTS.*

THE ONLY *LASTING* SOLUTION TO THE TENSION BETWEEN MANKIND AND THE MUTANT POPULATION IS A *PEACEFUL* ONE, STORM.

TURN YOUR BACK ON THIS GIRL NOW AND YOU MIGHT AS WELL SIGN UP WITH *MAGNETO.*

CYCLOPS?

I HATE TO SAY IT, BUT HE'S RIGHT.

WE *ALL* WANT TO SEE THE SENTINELS TAKEN OUT OF THE PICTURE, BUT WE CAN'T LET THE BROTHERHOOD USE THIS GIRL AS A *BARGAINING CHIP.*

I JUST HOPE YOU KNOW WHAT YOU'RE *DOING,* PROFESSOR.

WHAT ABOUT *YOU,* WOLVERINE? YOU TAGGING ALONG FOR OUR FIRST REAL FIGHT WITH THE BROTHERHOOD OF MUTANTS?

WELL, I KINDA HAD MY HEART SET ON PLAYIN' BACKGAMMON WITH THE *PROFESSOR* HERE, BUT WHY THE HECK NOT?

SOUNDS LIKE IT COULD BE A *LAUGH.*

CROATIA:

THIS STILL DOESN'T *SIT* RIGHT WITH ME, PEOPLE.

WHY DO I SUDDENLY FEEL LIKE A *BLACK GUY* DRAFTING NEWSLETTERS FOR THE *KU KLUX KLAN?*

I KNOW WHAT YOU MEAN, COLOSSUS, BUT THE PROFESSOR THINKS THIS IS OUR BEST CHANCE YET OF SHOWING THE PUBLIC THAT WE'RE NOT *ALL* PEOPLE-EATING MONSTERS.

BEAUTIFUL SENTIMENT, CYCLOPS, BUT I'M NOT COUNTING ANY CHICKENS.

IS ANYONE EVEN SURE WE'VE TRACKED THIS GIRL DOWN TO THE CORRECT *CONTINENT?*

OH, SHE'S HERE, STORM. CEREBRO WAS ABLE TO PINPOINT THE KIDNAPPERS RIGHT DOWN TO THE BRAND OF *TOILET PAPER* THEY'VE BEEN USING.

THEIR JET BACK TO THE SAVAGE LAND WON'T BE HERE FOR ANOTHER EIGHTEEN MINUTES, BUT I WANT EVERYBODY OUT OF THIS CREEPY, LITTLE COUNTRY WITH FIVE GIANT-SIZED MINUTES TO SPARE.

DOWN BELOW:

WHAT HAPPENED TO MY SODDING CIGARETTES? THERE WERE FIFTEEN IN THE PACK BEFORE I WENT FOR A SLASH.

I CAN SMOKE FIFTEEN BEFORE THE MATCH GOES OUT, TOAD. THIRTY IF I'M REALLY TRYING.

REALLY? WHAT A WONDERFUL MUTANT ABILITY, QUICKSILVER.

THANK GOD WE'VE GOT EACH OTHER FOR INTELLIGENT CONVERSATION, SCARLET WITCH.

ACTUALLY, THE ONLY INTELLIGENT CONVERSATION I GET AROUND HERE...

...IS WHEN I TALK TO MYSELF, MASTERMIND.

READY WHEN YOU ARE, COLOSSUS.

OH NO SHE ISN'T.

SHE'S COMING BACK TO THE SAVAGE LAND TO BE *HOUSE-TRAINED*, YOU TREACHEROUS PIECE OF FILTH.

I ALREADY PROMISED A LITTLE FISH-FACED *BOY* HE COULD KEEP THE HAIRLESS MONKEY AS A *PET*.

MISSING AN *ENGINE*, CYCLOPS?

MISSING A *FACE*, MORON?

YOU KNOW, WHOEVER SAID THAT TIGHT, LITTLE T-SHIRT DOESN'T MAKE YOU LOOK LIKE THE *TEAM PANSY* WAS *LYING,* CYCLOPS.

WAM

YOU'RE *NEXT,* BY THE WAY, YOU STUPID-LOOKING AMERICAN COW.

WHAT?

BEAST TO ALL POINTS: COLOSSUS AND I JUST DISABLED MASTERMIND AND THE BLOB --

WAM

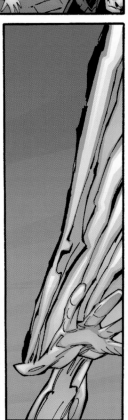

-- BUT MORE OF THEM ARE CRAWLING OUT OF THE WOODWORK EVERY *SECOND.* ANYONE FIT TO LEND A HAND?

SORRY, BEAST. PROBLEMS OF OUR *OWN* RIGHT NOW.

OH, BLOODY--

WOLVERINE TO MARVEL GIRL: CAN YOU READ MY MIND AND FLY THAT PLANE AT THE SAME TIME?

GET THE COFFEE ON, JEAN. I'LL BE WITH YOU IN A SECOND.

LOUD AND CLEAR, WOLVERINE, BUT THE COMPUTER SAYS THE ONLY WAY WE CAN PULL THIS OFF IS IF YOU GET THAT HEAP UP TO A HUNDRED AND TWENTY.

WOLVERINE, THIS IS CYCLOPS: WHAT ARE YOU DOING?

AROUND A HUNDRED AND FRIGGIN' TWENTY, I HOPE.

YOU'D DO ANYTHING TO IMPRESS A SEVENTEEN-YEAR-OLD IN A TIGHT SWEATER, WOULDN'T YOU?

ACTUALLY, I'VE KINDA GOT MY EYE ON A TELEPATHIC *NINETEEN*-YEAR-OLD, BUT I'M WORRIED SHE'S GONNA WASTE HER LIFE WAITING ON A LOSER WHO BRUSHES HIS *TEETH* SIX TIMES A DAY.

DON'T GIVE UP HOPE, WOLVERINE.

YOU NEVER KNOW YOUR LUCK.

CYCLOPS TO MARVEL GIRL: GIVE YOURSELF A PAT ON THE BACK AND RENDEZVOUS FIVE MILES WEST AS PLANNED, JEAN.

OH, AND *WOLVERINE* --?

-- NICE WORK.

BAD NEWS, PEOPLE: THE BROTHERHOOD'S PLANE JUST TOUCHED DOWN FOR THE *SAVAGE LAND* TRIP WITH A GUY IN A PURPLE CAPE WHO LOOKS *DISTURBINGLY* FAMILIAR.

MAGNETO?

THIS JUST GETS WORSE BY THE *SECOND.* DROP WHO YOU'RE *HITTING* AND START *RUNNING,* BOYS AND GIRLS.

WE DID WHAT WE WERE *ASKED* TO DO; NOW LETS GET *OUT* WHILE WE'RE ALL STILL PACKING A *PULSE.*

WE'RE *TOO LATE,* CYCLOPS.

WHAT ARE YOU *TALKING* ABOUT?

ACTUALLY, I CAN HARDLY BELIEVE CHARLES SENT YOU HERE MYSELF.

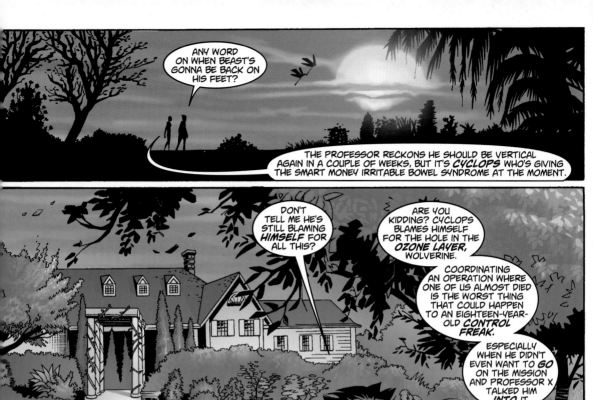

ANY WORD ON WHEN BEAST'S GONNA BE BACK ON HIS FEET?

THE PROFESSOR RECKONS HE SHOULD BE VERTICAL AGAIN IN A COUPLE OF WEEKS, BUT IT'S *CYCLOPS* WHO'S GIVING THE SMART MONEY IRRITABLE BOWEL SYNDROME AT THE MOMENT.

DON'T TELL ME HE'S STILL BLAMING *HIMSELF* FOR ALL THIS?

ARE YOU KIDDING? CYCLOPS BLAMES HIMSELF FOR THE HOLE IN THE *OZONE LAYER,* WOLVERINE.

COORDINATING AN OPERATION WHERE ONE OF US ALMOST DIED IS THE WORST THING THAT COULD HAPPEN TO AN EIGHTEEN-YEAR-OLD *CONTROL FREAK.*

ESPECIALLY WHEN HE DIDN'T EVEN WANT TO *GO* ON THE MISSION AND PROFESSOR X TALKED HIM *INTO* IT.

HE FEELS LIKE A FIRST-CLASS *IDIOT.*

WHAT ABOUT *YOU*? HOW DO *YOU* FEEL?

RATTLED. BUT I TRUST THE PROFESSOR, AND THE LATEST FROM WASHINGTON IS THAT THE PRESIDENT'S FEELING HIGHLY CONCILIATORY SINCE HE GOT HIS *DAUGHTER* BACK.

THE PROFESSOR EXPECTS A SUSPENSION OF THE SENTINEL PROGRAM IN THE NEXT SIXTY TO NINETY *MINUTES.*

NO, JEAN. HOW DO YOU FEEL ABOUT *ME*?

HONESTLY?

I'M NOT SURE I PARTICULARLY *LIKE* YOU, WOLVERINE.

SURE, YOU'VE PROVED YOURSELF AS AN X-MAN, BUT I HAVEN'T *BOUGHT* THIS IDEA THAT YOU'RE AN OVERNIGHT CONVERT TO PROFESSOR XAVIER'S INTEGRATIONIST IDEOLOGY.

YOUR WEAPON X TRAINING MIGHT MEAN I CAN'T READ THE THOUGHTS YOU DON'T *WANT* ME TO, BUT I'M EMPATHIC ENOUGH TO KNOW YOU'RE HERE FOR ALL THE WRONG REASONS.

I THINK THE WAY PEOPLE HAVE TREATED YOU OVER THE YEARS HAS REALLY SCREWED YOU UP, AND AS MUCH AS IT GOES AGAINST EVERYTHING THE SCHOOL'S SUPPOSED TO STAND FOR --

-- I REALLY, REALLY WISH WE'D NEVER *MET* YOU.

SO HOW COME YOU FIND ME SO *ATTRACTIVE?*

I WISH I KNEW.

CAN YOU READ WHAT I'M THINKING *NOW*, PROFESSOR?

LANGUAGE LIKE *THAT* BETRAYS A LIMITED VOCABULARY, CYCLOPS.

WELL, RIGHT NOW I'M FEELING *MONOSYLLABIC*, MAN.

GIVE ME A CALL WHEN YOU GET TIRED OF SUCKING UP TO THE *EVIL EMPIRE*.

BEAST TO ALL AVAILABLE X-MEN. I REPEAT, THIS IS BEAST CALLING ANY X-MEN CURRENTLY ON THE PREMISES --

WOULD SOMEBODY COME ALONG TO THE INFIRMARY AND EXPLAIN WHY I'VE SUDDENLY GOT *BLUE HAIR?*

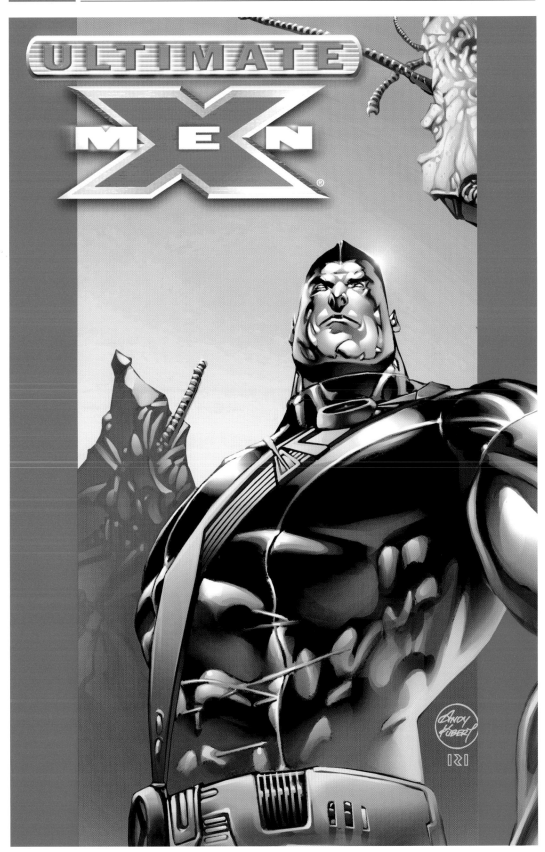

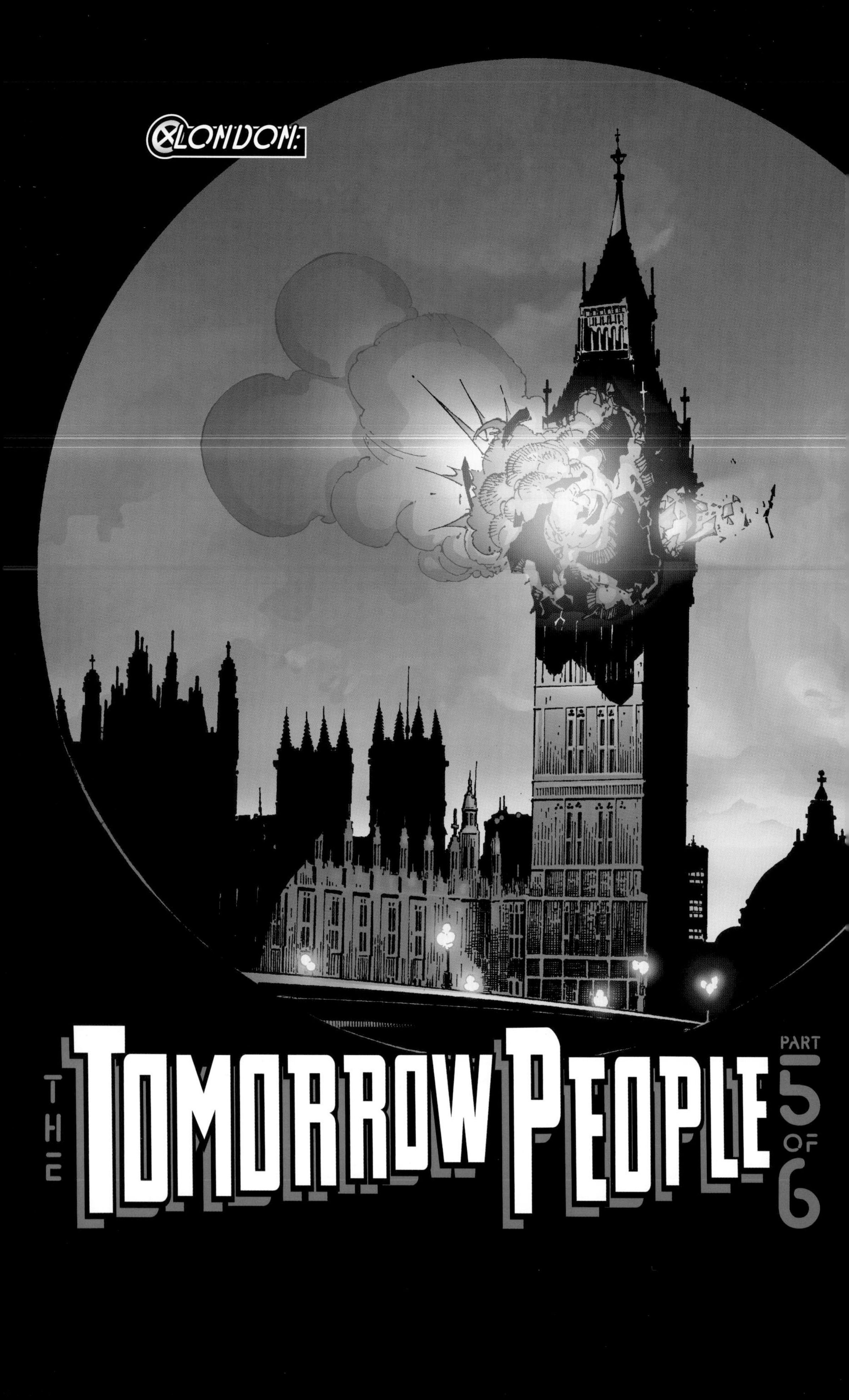
LONDON:
THE TOMORROW PEOPLE
PART 5 OF 6

EVERYONE PRETTY MUCH AGREES THAT *NEGOTIATIONS* ARE THE BEST WAY FORWARD NOW, BUT THERE'S STILL ONE, FINAL MISSION PLANNED FOR BOLIVAR TRASK'S MACHINES, I'M AFRAID.

I'M NOT SURE I FOLLOW YOU, SIR.

THE *SAVAGE LAND*, PROFESSOR.

WE FINALLY UNCOVERED ITS *WHEREABOUTS.*

OH MY GOD.

TO BE HONEST, WE'D PROBABLY NEVER HAVE FOUND IT IF IT HADN'T BEEN FOR THE *BLACKBIRD JET* OUR SATELLITES PICKED UP LANDING IN THE AREA A COUPLE OF WEEKS AGO.

IT WAS ONLY ONCE WE LOOKED A LITTLE CLOSER THAT WE REALIZED THAT WHAT SEEMED LIKE A SCATTERED ROCK FORMATION WAS ACTUALLY JUST A COMPLEX, THREE- DIMENSIONAL *HOLOGRAM.*

WAY TO GO, CYCLOPS.

QUIET, STORM.

DOES THIS MEAN YOU'RE PREPARING AN ATTACK?

YOU LOOK TROUBLED, CYCLOPS.

MAYBE I'M JUST NOT AS THRILLED ABOUT *KILLING* PEOPLE AS THE GUYS I SHARE A BATHROOM WITH AT THE MOMENT, MAGNETO.

BUT YOU DIDN'T KILL *ANYONE*, SCOTT. QUICKSILVER ALWAYS DETONATES THE BOMBS.

I HEAR HE HOPES THESE DISPLAYS OF PUBLIC CRUELTY MIGHT BRING US CLOSER TOGETHER, BUT IT'S *QUITE THE REVERSE*, I'M AFRAID.

MAN IS *ALONE* AMONG THE ANIMALS WHEN IT COMES TO TAKING PLEASURE IN THE SUFFERING OF OTHERS.

HOMO SUPERIOR LOVES *ALL* LIVING THINGS.

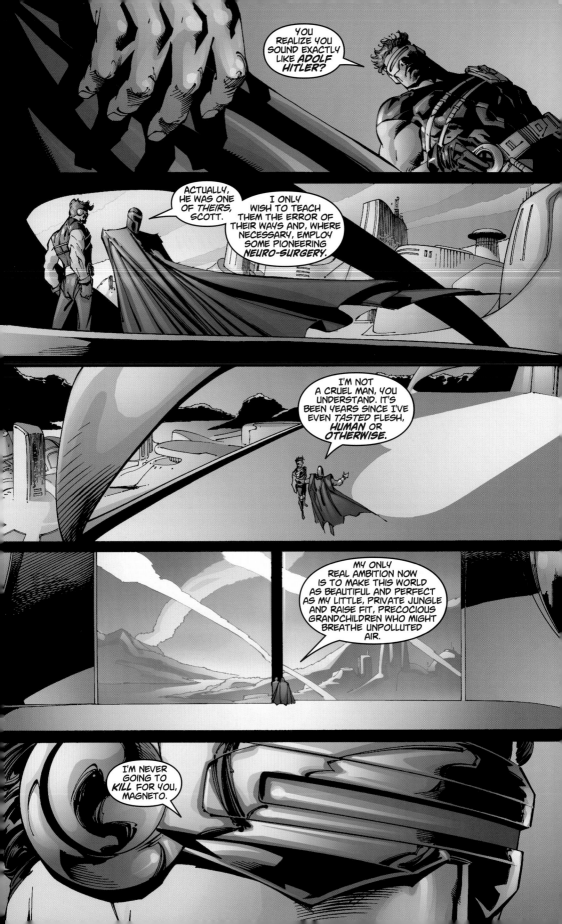

WHY DOES HE TAKE SUCH PLEASURE IN *HURTING* ME, WANDA?

HAVE I REALLY BEEN SUCH A BAD SON THAT I DESERVE TO CRY MYSELF TO SLEEP LIKE THIS EVERY NIGHT?

MAGNETO COULDN'T *ASK* FOR A MORE PERFECT SON, PIETRO.

BLOB SAYS HE JUST RESENTS US BECAUSE WE'RE CONSTANT, LIVING REMINDERS OF HIS ONE MOMENT OF WEAKNESS WITH A *HOMO SAPIEN* FEMALE ALL THOSE YEARS AGO.

BUT I WISH HE'D STOP CRITICIZING ME IN FRONT OF PEOPLE. HE EVEN SAID MY MUTANT POWER WAS *EFFEMINATE* THIS MORNING.

POOR PIETRO -- EVEN WHEN YOU WERE A LITTLE BOY, ALL YOU EVER WANTED WAS TO MAKE HIM *PROUD.*

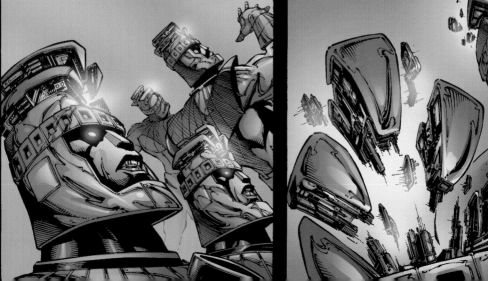

F-FATHER?

WHAT ARE YOU DOING?

WHAT DOES IT LOOK LIKE I'M DOING, YOU IMBECILE? I'M REARRANGING THEIR CIRCUIT BOARDS.

CHANGING THEIR PRIME DIRECTIVE FROM HUNTING AND KILLING ANYONE WITH MUTANT GENES TO HUNTING AND KILLING ANYONE WITHOUT THEM.

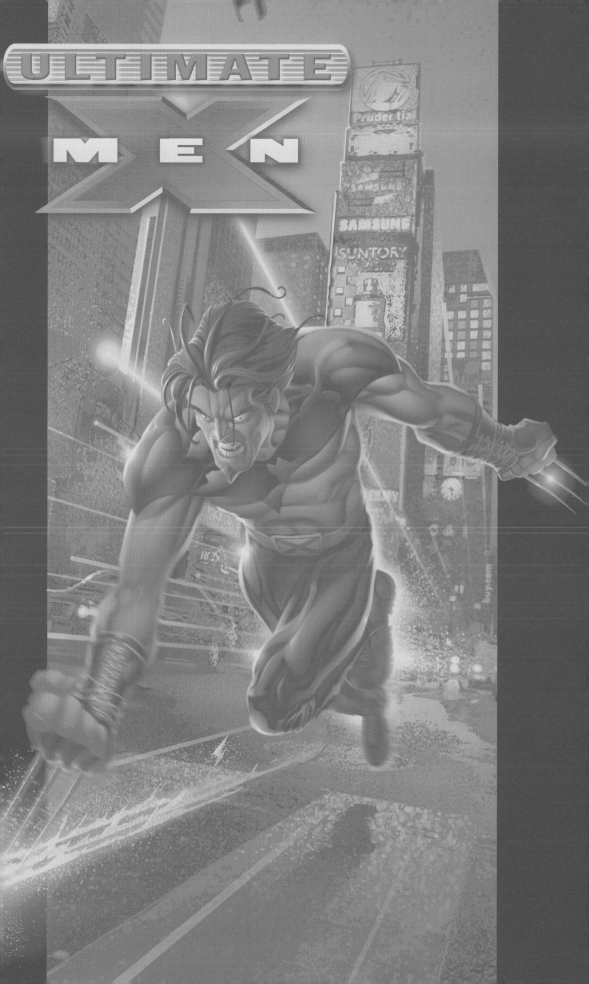

OH MY GOD! THE PROFESSOR'S HAVING SOME KIND OF *SEIZURE.* I THINK HIS *BRAIN'S* CLOSING DOWN.

DON'T *TOUCH* HIM, PETER. HE JUST NEEDS ANOTHER FEW SECONDS IN MAGNETO'S HEAD--

--TO PULL THIS THING *OFF.*

GOODBYE, OLD FRIEND. GIVE MY *REGARDS* TO THE *DODO.*

IT'S GOOD TO HAVE YOU *BACK*, CYCLOPS.

THE XAVIER INSTITUTE FOR GIFTED CHILDREN

IT'S GOOD TO *BE* BACK, SIR. I'M JUST GLAD I DIDN'T LET EVERYONE DOWN TOO MUCH BY STORMING *OUT* OF HERE LIKE THAT.

NOT AT ALL, SCOTT. YOU WERE THERE WHEN YOU WERE NEEDED AND THAT'S THE ONLY THING THAT MATTERS.

THIS ENTIRE EPISODE HAS WORKED OUT PRECISELY AS I WOULD HAVE WANTED.

EVEN WOLVERINE?

--ALTHOUGH, FROM WHAT I HEAR, HE'S LEAVING IN THE MORNING TO TAKE CARE OF SOME UNFINISHED BUSINESS *ELSEWHERE*.

REALLY? I HADN'T *HEARD.*

DON'T LOOK TOO *DISAPPOINTED*, MR. SUMMERS.

AS FAR AS I'M CONCERNED, WOLVERINE HAS *MORE* THAN PROVED HIMSELF AS AN X-MAN, YOUNG SCOTT.

HE'S AS WELCOME IN THESE CORRIDORS AS ANYONE --